OPTICAL ILLUSION MAGIC

VISUAL TRICKS & AMUSEMENTS

Michael A. DiSpezio

Sterling Publishing Co., Inc.
New York

Acknowledgments

My experience with the Sterling Publishing Company has once again celebrated an often-obscured truth in publishing: Most authors owe their success to the hard work, talent, support, and capabilities of their behind-the-lines army.

Once again, I'd like to thank Sheila Barry for having faith in my project proposal. I'd also like to recognize an unseen helper who has until now remained "unmentioned" in all of my Sterling projects: John Woodside, Editorial Director. From uncovering errors in my puzzling logic to discovering oversights in my impossible figures, John has been there to share his insight, experience, and passion for publishing excellence. Without visuals, there can be no optical magic. My magnificent and multitalented artists were Jeffrey Ward and Myron Miller. Finally, I want to recognize a very special and talented person, Hazel Chan. I have had the honor to work with this dedicated, always upbeat, and overall wonderful person on seven books. Seven books! Where does the time go? With each new project, Hazel infuses her positive outlook and editorial skills into the pages of a book whose cover will identify me as author. Thanks, Hazel.

Permissions for Optical Illusions: Page 13, Color-blind test chart: J. Creamer, MD http://www.colorblindtest.com; Page 14, Astigmatism chart courtesy of Carolina Biological Supply Company carolina@carolina.com; Page 72: Pattern of Saturns: photo NASA/JPL/Caltech; Page 77: Red/blue 5 tetrahedra stereoimage created by Mark Newbold at www.sover.net/~manx; Page 77: Anaglyph of suspension bridge at Darjeeling, India: Keystone-Mast Collection, UCR/California Museum of Photography, University of California, Riverside; Pages 78–79: All Mars anaglyph photos by NASA/JPL/Caltech.

Library of Congress Cataloging-in-Publication Data Available

DiSpezio, Michael A.
   Optical illusion magic : visual tricks & amusements / Michael DiSpezio
     p. cm.
    ISBN 0-8069-6581-9
    1. Optical illusions.
   QP495.D573   1999
   152.14'8—DC21   99-21113
                              CIP

10 9 8 7 6 5 4 3

First paperback edition published 2001 by
Sterling Publishing Company, Inc.
387 Park Avenue South, New York, N.Y. 10016
© 1999 by Michael A. DiSpezio
Distributed in Canada by Sterling Publishing
c/o Canadian Manda Group, One Atlantic Avenue, Suite 105
Toronto, Ontario, Canada M6K 3E7
Distributed in Great Britain and Europe by Chris Lloyd at Orca Book
Services, Stanley House, Fleets Lane, Poole BH15 3AJ, England
Distributed in Australia by Capricorn Link (Australia) Pty Ltd.
P.O. Box 704, Windsor, NSW 2756, Australia
Printed in China
All rights reserved

Sterling ISBN 0-8069-6581-9 Trade
           0-8069-6627-0 Paper

Contents

Introduction

Illusions are cool. It doesn't matter what age you are. People are always drawn to their magic and eye-popping "wow." Prior to the publication of this book, there were two types of illusion books. One type of book was a coffee table showpiece. Its pages were stocked with illusion after illusion. Although this type of colorful collection was "candy for the eyes," it did little to explain why these illusions occurred.

The other type of book was more "cerebral." With a title such as *Neocortical Processing of Subliminal Kinetic Effects*, the mostly stark pages had scant illustrations. At best, the images were ancillary drawings that helped explain a limited number of visual tricks. So unless you were a graduate student in experimental psychology, you probably wouldn't be reading this kind of publication. Enter this book, *Optical Illusion Magic*. Within these eye-popping, mind-building pages, you'll discover the best of both worlds-entertainment with education that is explained in plain old English.

Short Cuts

Do you like to take short-cuts? Everyone does. In fact, you are right now taking all sorts of shortcuts-most of which you are not even aware of! The shortcuts I'm talking about won't get you to the movies quicker. They won't even slice through math problems. They will, however, help your brain make "quick" sense of the world around you.

TRICKY TRACKS

Take a look at the two dinosaurs. A good look! The dinosaur at the top of the tracks appears to be slightly larger than the animal at the bottom of the picture. Right? Wrong. As you'll see, appearances can be deceiving.

You may need a ruler to check this out, but the two dinosaurs are the exact same size! Your brain followed the wrong short-cut and got lost. It wound up in the state of confusion (very close to the District of Columbia).

AN EXTRA TREAT

Get two identical animal cookies. Place one cookie over each dinosaur. Is the railroad track effect strong enough to make these objects look different? Try placing pairs of other identical objects such as checkers, chips, and coins on the tracks. Does the background also affect the size of these objects?

PICTURE THIS

The railroad track illusion also works with a photograph. Both horizontal bars are the exact same size and length! Those same misleading clues (also called cues) are at it again.

CLASSICAL CONNECTION
This illusion, called the Ponzo illusion, first appeared in 1913. Both red lines are identical. Can you see the similarities between this drawing and the railroad track foolery?

WHAT HAPPENED? Okay, who did it? Who printed the portrait of the Mona Lisa upside down?

Since our lady is in this flipped-out mood, let's take advantage of it. Take a good look her. Is she happy or sad? Is she looking directly at you or slightly to your left? Are you sure?

Spin the book around so that she's right-side up. Wow!

You were tricked! Remember the shortcut concept? When you were faced with an upside-down view, your brain was "ultra"- challenged! It used all of the shortcuts it could in order to make sense of what it was seeing.

In figuring out that this image was a human face, your brain was too busy to make sure all of the face parts were pointing in the right direction. When you spun the face to its right-side-up position, your brain was much less stressed. It had time to realize that something was odd—very odd. Her eyes and mouth were turned upside down!

Highlight

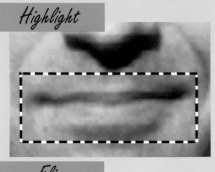

Flip

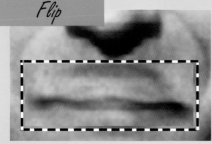

Smudge

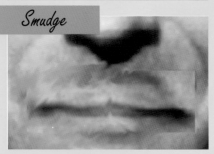

Impress Your Friends!

You can make a crazy upside-down head shot just like this one. All you need is access to a computer graphics program, a photo, and a scanner. Scan your picture (or take a new one with a digital camera). Open the picture in a graphics program. Highlight the eyes and mouth. Use the flip command to spin around these face parts. To soften edges, you may want to smudge or smooth the borders.

Magazine Madness Even without a computer, you can create this illusion. Get an old fashion magazine that has pages filled with faces. Select a face that looks straight at you. Tear this page out. Carefully cut out the eye and mouth regions. Spin these pieces around and replace them. Use tape on the backside of the page to secure these inserts. Turn the page upside down and you're ready for the face foolery challenge.

Illusion Basics

Which line appears longer, AB or CD?

Although they may not look it, AB and CD are the same exact length. It's the arrowheads and tails at work. They trick your brain into "seeing" something that appears different from what it actually is. That's called an "illusion"!

What causes this illusion? No one can say for certain, but many psychologists (scientists who study illusions) believe it has to do with things you've seen before. AB may remind you of the near edge of a building. CD may remind you of a distant wall.

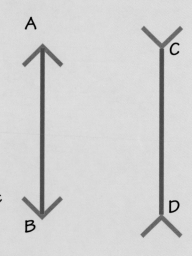

What's the Story with AB?

When you look at the corner of a building, the nearest edge projects a longer line than the other corners. From experience, however, you know that all corners of the building must be the same height.

What happens? It's all part of your brain's "tweaking," in which it slightly alters an image. In this case, your brain performs an automatic "shrink" and reduces the height of this near edge.

What's the Story with CD?

When you look at a distant wall, that edge projects a shorter length than the nearby corners. From experience, however, you know that all corners are the same height. Your brain performs an automatic "stretch" to this edge.

AB + CD = ?

When you look at the complete illusion, both automatic adjustments are at work. While AB shrinks, CD stretches. The result is a confused comparison.

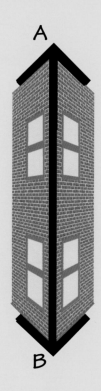

SIDEWAYS TOO

The trick based upon the arrowhead and tail add-ons is called the Muller-Leyer illusion. Franz Muller-Leyer devised this illusion back in 1889. The Muller-Leyer illusion can be presented in several different ways. Suppose we combine the two line-segments into a single line. Does the illusion still work?

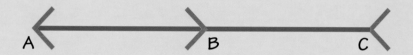

You bet it does! Your brain automatically shrinks AB while at the same time it stretches the appearance of BC.

SPACE RETAINER

Examine the spaces between the dots. Is the distance between the red and green dots the same as the distance between the green and blue dots?

Even without lines, the arrowheads are strong enough to suggest clues that lead us astray. The distance between the red dot and green dot is less than the distance between the green dot and blue dot. Those false clues are at it again. They stretch the distance on the left. At the same time, they trick you into shortening the distance on the right.

INTO THE POOL

Examine the three sets of racked pool balls. See the black ball? Great, easy to do, and no tricks. Examine the distance from this black ball to the yellow ball (length AB) and the black ball to the red ball (length BC). Which appears longer, AB or BC?

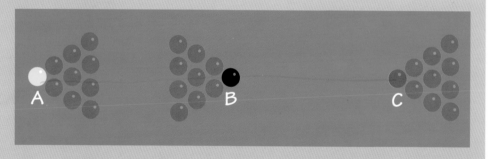

Strange, but true—AB is slightly longer. It's the Muller-Leyer illusion with a "racked-up" twist.

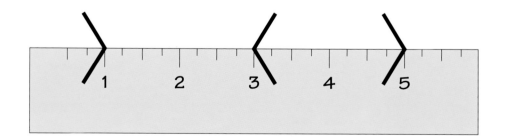

Would a ruler help you compare lengths? Give it a try. Which two inches appears longer?

Bending the Rules

Rules, rules, and more rules. Throughout your life, your brain has constructed a type of rule book filled with all sorts of tricks to help you "see faster." These shortcuts are used to deal with the incredible amount of information detected by your eyes. Without shortcuts, there would be too much information, and your brain would get stuck trying to separate the important things from the visual garbage.

Take a look at the image below. You've probably seen it before. It's based upon the Hering illusion, which was first published in 1861. Around that time, astronomers and stargazers had an interest in optical illusions. They wanted to learn how their vision could be fooled when looking through a telescope.

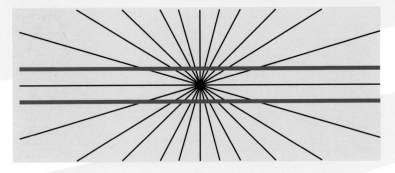

Although they don't appear it, the blue lines remain straight and parallel across their entire lengths. You can verify this by placing a ruler along the lines.

Look below. These two blue lines are also parallel. The concept was conceived and studied by Wilhelm Wundt in 1896.

What's the Trick?

The trick comes from the background pattern. This pattern contains an arrangement of lines that reminds your brain of something it has seen before—two surfaces forming a bend.

Your brain quickly takes this shortcut and "constructs" an image of a bend that appears to fold outward along its horizontal midline. This construction of depth is so strong that it changes the way you see other parts of the image. Lines that are placed over the pattern become "warped" to fit the imagined depth.

BENT PENCILS

Place three pencils (or straws) atop this pattern. Their points and erasers should be positioned as shown. Does the background pattern change the appearance of the pencils?

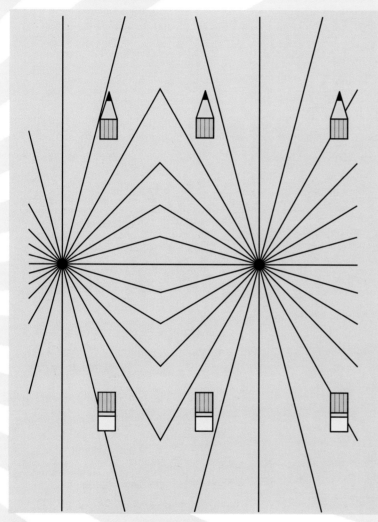

Straight Answers

The background pattern is at it again—reminding your brain of familiar slanting surfaces. This memory is strong enough to "warp" anything placed on top of these lines. Even though the pencils remain straight, they take on a bent appearance to fit your brain's case of mistaken identity.

RUBBER PENCILS

Here's another way to "bend" a rigid pencil. Hold the end of the pencil between your thumb and index finger. The pencil should be positioned so that it can swing up and down while being gently held by your fingers. Move your hand up and down while allowing the pencil to sway back and forth. Observers will "see" a pencil bending as if it were rubber.

This bending has nothing to do with a background pattern. The rubbery look is caused by the double motion of the pencil. Your brain has trouble keeping the up-and-down and back-and-forth movement separate. In its confused state, it constructs a rubber-like pencil that sways up and down.

Illusions and the Eye

Some types of visual tricks depend upon the way your eyes and brain are hooked up. Hold this page about 1 foot from your face. Close one eye and stare at the bull's-eye below. Note how you can still see the star even though you are not looking directly at it. Keep looking at the bull's-eye with one eye while you slowly move your face closer and closer to the page. At a certain distance, the star disappears.

What Happened to the Star?

Was it sucked up by a black hole? Was it transported to another galaxy through a worm hole? Hardly. It was an accepted casualty of the "blind spot."

The blind spot is a small area on your eye's light sensitive screen. As its name suggests, this spot is blind! It lacks the light-detecting cells needed to see things.

Location. Location. Location. The reason that the blind spot has no light detectors is because of its location. The spot is found right on the point where the optic nerve hooks up to the eye.

To get a better idea of how the eye is put together, you might want to check out the drawing on the next page.

THINK ABOUT IT

Perhaps you are wondering why blind spots don't interfere with your vision? The answer has to do with us having two eyes. Each eye has a different blind spot. Your brain just takes the image from the eye and uses it to "fill" the blind spot of the other eye.

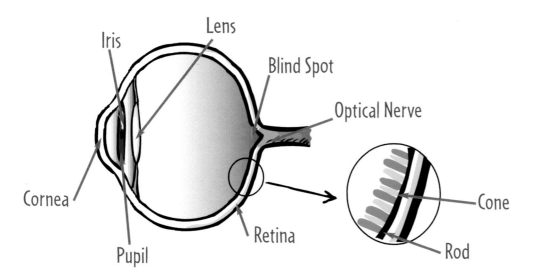

Iris
Lens
Blind Spot
Optical Nerve
Cornea
Cone
Pupil
Retina
Rod

COLOR CONFUSION

People who are color-blind have problems in detecting or distinguishing colors. The test on the right can be used to screen for a type of color blindness. Can you see the shapes in this jumble of dots?

Night Vision If you want to see a dim star at night, don't look directly at it. Look off to its side. Why? It has to do with the concentration of rods. Rods are not concentrated at the center of the retina. Instead, they are found off center. Therefore, if you look slightly to one side of the star, its faint light will fall on a more light-sensitive region of the retina.

Lens: clear muscle. By changing its shape, the lens can focus images on the eye's light-sensitive screen.

Iris: muscular disk that changes size depending upon the brightness of a scene. Your eye color depends upon the pigments in this muscle.

Pupil: dark spot in the middle of the iris. Light travels through this opening to get inside the eye.

Retina: light-sensitive layer of the eye. This is the "screen" on which the lens focuses its image.

Rods: very sensitive light-detecting cells. Although they can detect dim light, they cannot distinguish different colors.

Cones: only detect bright light. Unlike the rods, cones can distinguish colors.

Optic nerve: a bundle of nerve fibers that move messages from the eye to the brain.

Blind spot: where the optic nerve joins the retina. There are no light-sensitive cells in this region.

Eye Tricks

Blind spots aren't the only cool tricks you can "see" with your eyes. Shut one eye and examine the pattern below. Which set of lines looks darker? Are you sure? Rotate the page one quarter turn. Which set looks darker now?

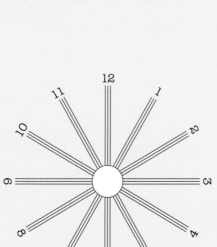

FINGER FOOD Here's how to make a floating finger hot dog. Stare past your fingers as you touch the tips of your index fingers. What do you see? Slowly pull your fingers apart. What happens?

The floating hot dog was created by an overlap of images. Each eye had a separate view. The part of the finger that was seen by both eyes appeared as a separate piece floating between the fingertips. Look at the floating finger hot dog as you shut one eye, then the other. Can you see both edges of the hot dog formed by fingertips?

Astigma-what?

Astigmatism (pronounced Ah-STIG-mah-tizz-um). It's an eye problem that results in a region of poor focus. Most of us have a slight degree of astigmatism. A chart such as this one is used by eye doctors to uncover and measure the disorder. As you probably figured out, all of these lines are identical. The difference in darkness is from focus problems.

HAND OUT Roll a sheet of paper into a tube. Hold the tube next to your hand. Keep both eyes open and look through the tube and at your hand. What do you see?

Hole-ee One eye sees a hand. The other eye sees down the tube. Most of the time a two-eyed view produces a wide view. This time, it created an optical illusion.

TWO-EYED SHOT

Hold this image about a foot away from your nose. Stare at the letter X. Now slowly bring this page closer to your nose.

Score! Basketball in the hoop! This illusion also has to do with different views seen by each eye. At a critical distance, the right and left eye images come together and the ball appears in the hoop.

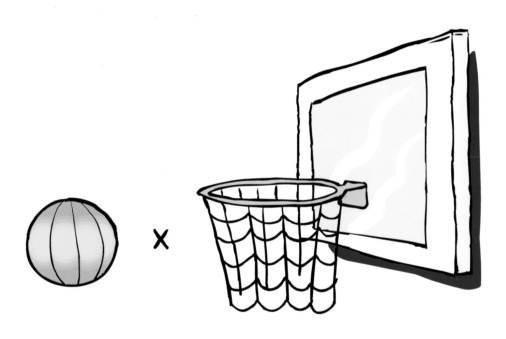

CONNECTIONS

Take a look at the facing page. It is a list of different-color words. Each word is printed in a color of ink that is different from the color spelled by its letters. Red is printed in blue ink. Green is printed in black ink. Easy.

THE CHALLENGE Your challenge is to identify the colors of ink (not the spelled words) that are used to print the letters of each word. I'll help you out. For the first line, you'll say: Blue. Black. Green. Red.

Now, it's your turn. Hold the page at arm's length. Start off with the words on the top line and continue quickly along the list.

What Happened? Dribble mouth. Your brain is divided up into different regions. Each region has its own task. One region specializes in language (which includes spelling and understanding the meaning of words). Another region's specialty is identifying colors.

When you looked at the first word, each region "saw" something different. The language part read the word. It saw the letters R, E, and D. It put them together into a familiar three-letter word and recognized "red," a word that represents a color. This part of the brain generated a message that said red, red, red, red.

The color processing part didn't care about the letters or what they spelled. It concentrated on the ink's color. It recognized the color of ink as "blue." This part of the brain generated a message which said blue, blue, blue.

When the two messages arrived at another processing region, the brain was faced with two different things to say. This created confusion.

red green pink yellow
blue violet green grey
orange black purple
red green pink yellow
blue violet green grey
orange black purple

SPADIX VIRIDIS FULVUS
CROCEUS RUBER FUCUS
PUNICEUS CAERULEUS
VIRIDUS FLAVUS SPADIX

TONGUE UN-TIED

Here's a slightly different version of the color words. This time, the words aren't spelled in English. They're in Latin. Do you think that you'll still have the same confusion? Why or why not?

17

Only the Shadow Knows

Which way is the Sun? Overhead.

Which way is the ceiling light? Overhead.

Which way is the street light? Overhead.

Which way is the full moon? Overhead.

Most of the time, light comes from above. Sure, it can come from the side or even from below on dance floors. But, generally, light comes from overhead. The "lofty" position of light leads to several visual cues. Some of these cues appear to be instinct. They are "hard-wired" into our brain at birth. Other clues seem to be added to our brain's rule book from everyday experiences.

Do you see the dents below? Great. Like all dents, they bend into the material. Can you figure out the direction of light that fell upon these dents when the picture was snapped? Good. Remember that.

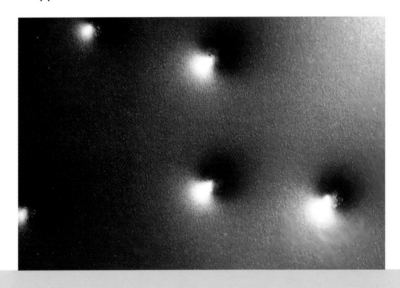

Hold on to this page. Close your eyes. Spin this page upside down. Open your eyes. What happens to the dents? Most likely, they changed into little bumps. They now appear to come "out" of the material.

Spin the page back and the dents return. Is this illusion strong enough to produce the transformation with eyes open? Dents to bumps. Bumps to dents. Dents to bumps.

What Causes the Change?

This "flipping" is due to your brain's "fixing" on the light's direction. Hold the page upright. Look at one of the circular marks. Your brain assumes that when this picture was taken the light came from above. It illuminated the lower half of the mark while the upper half re-mained in shadow. From experience, you've learned that this type of lighting is found on dents!

Spin the page around. Your brain is more concerned with keeping the overhead light direction than keeping the image consistent. As the image spun around, your brain reanalyzed what it saw. The marks now had light on the top while the bottoms were in shadow. From experience, you've learned that this type of lighting is found on bumps!

TIME FOR A BREAK

How about some dessert? There seems to be enough cheesecake for everyone.

Spin this page upside down and what happens to the pie? Almost all of it disappears, leaving only a single slice of cheesecake!

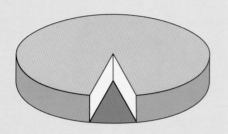

Who Ate the Pie?

This illusion is also produced by light cues. In the upright position, it made sense to see an almost complete cheesecake that was missing rather than a single slice. When flipped upside down, the lit surfaces suggested a slightly different pie. Under this new lighting, it was more logical to "see" a single piece within an almost empty pie pan.

EXTRA FUN

Have you ever placed a flashlight beneath your chin and switched it on? If so, you produced a pretty weird look! So weird that you might not have even recognized yourself! Try it and look in a mirror!

Your uneasy appearance has to do with unfamiliar lighting cues. When your brain sees this oddly lit face, there's little it can do. There is no simple "tweaking" to make the light come from above. It accepts that the object is a face, but knows that this is very unnatural. Often, people will associate a sinister or evil mood with this reversed light direction. Watch for this lighting trick in movies and plays!

BLOCK STACKS

How many blocks do you see in the stack at the right? Six, right? Three in the bottom level, two in the middle level, and one on top. Great.

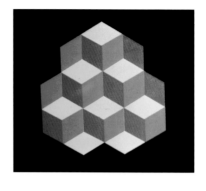

Flip this page upside down. How many blocks do you see now? Seven? Where did the extra block come from?

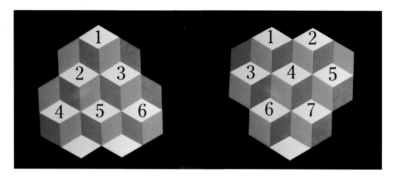

As you probably guessed, it had to do with lighting. Your brain assumes that light comes from above. As light strikes an object, it makes its upper surface bright. Therefore, your brain uses the brightest surfaces as a "handle" to count blocks. The rest of the image was made to fit these surfaces.

The upright page had six surfaces that were bright and, therefore, likely tops. When the book was turned upside down, seven possible tops appeared. Your brain rebuilt the image to fit this count.

Spots Before Your Eyes

Take a look at the pattern of black squares below. Most likely you'll observe spots that appear at the corners. But these spots don't seem to stick around. There's no problem in seeing them at the corners of your vision. But what happens when you try to look and focus directly on one of these spots?

The Disappearing Act Explained—Somewhat

This type of illusion seems to be based upon communication between light-detecting cells. When a cell is stimulated by light, it sends messages to the surrounding cells. These messages change the way neighboring cells respond to light. This change enhances the edges of an image, making an object's outline easier to see.

White that lies between the sides of two black blocks is "pumped up." This effect makes the white line segments seem brighter. White that is found at intersections lacks the side-by-side black border. Your brain does not "pump up" this white and therefore it appears less bright. The reduced brightness of these white regions makes them appear as gray spots.

The cells that produce this effect are concentrated away from the center of the retina. That's why the spots appear to disappear when you look right at them!

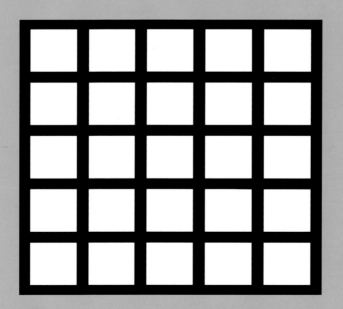

THINGS AREN'T ALWAYS WHITE AND BLACK

Suppose we reversed the pattern. Would you still see spots if the blocks were white and the lines printed in black? Make a guess. Then fix your vision on the pattern at the left.

SPOTS OF A DIFFERENT COLOR

Look at the red and green blocks at the right. What color spots dance at the corners of pattern?

MACH TOO   As you've seen, the "pumping up" of edges can create spots where there are no spots. This enhancement can also produce illusionary lines. Named after the discoverer, Mach bands form between regions of different brightness.

Hold this page at arm's length. Look at the patterns on the left. How are they similar? How are they different?

The purple pattern produces a bright Mach band. The lines left of center are uniform. To the right, they become wider.

The green pattern produces a dark Mach band. The lines right of center are uniform. To the left, they become thinner.

The Circle Game

Circles are great subjects for visual tricks. Why? Because their rounded edges keep eyes moving. Since your eyes can't fix on a distinct point, their shifting reference sets the scene for some great eye tricks.

Look at circle below. Which color dot is placed at the center of the circle?

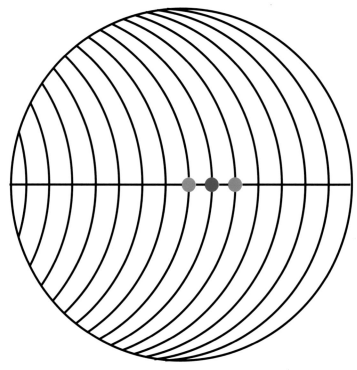

It doesn't look it, but the red dot is in the exact center. The curves trick us into thinking that the center is to the right of where it actually is!

FLAT ON THE GROUND? Take a look at the position of these circles. Are they arranged on a straight line or do they arch up in the middle?

On the Edge If you place a ruler along the bottom edge of the circles, you'll discover that all of the shapes lie on a flat, straight line. The arching is an illusion produced by your eye's difficulty in fixing on one distinct spot.

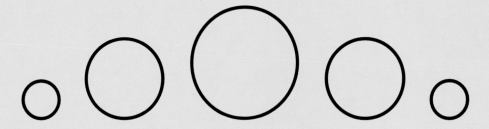

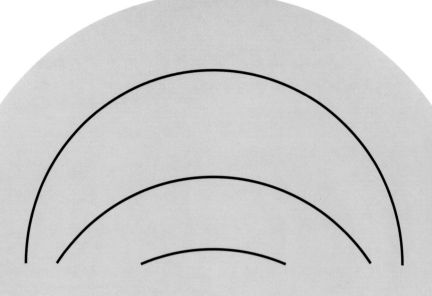

ANOTHER CURVE BALL

Examine the curved lines on the left. All three arcs are sections that have been removed from circles. Are any of the arcs taken from the same circle? If so, which ones?

They all belong to the same-sized circle. Hard to believe, but it's true!

THE PLOT THICKENS (AND SO DO THE CURVES)

Examine the curved shapes to the right. Okay, so one of them is bigger. But, by how much? Make a guess, then check your answer below.

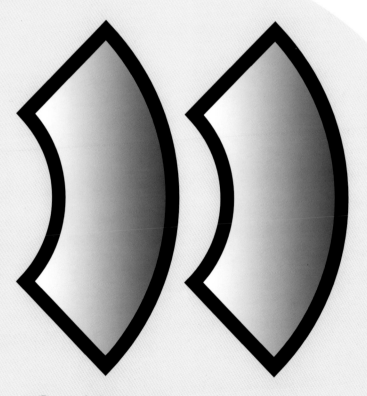

Get Your Ruler

Both shapes are the exact same size. Your brain's measuring system follows misleading curves that trick it into seeing things that just aren't so!

23

SPIRAL BOUND

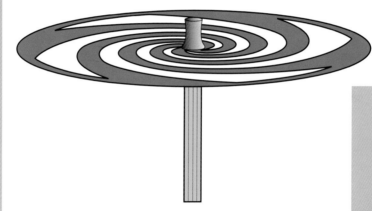

Photocopy the spiral pattern on this page. Paste the copy on a backing of heavy stock paper. Use a pair of scissors to trim away the excess paper. Position the eraser of a pencil beneath the center of the disk. Inset a push pin through the top of the disk so that it secures the spiral through its center point. The disk should spin freely.

Stare at the center of the spiral. Slowly spin the disk in one direction. What happens to the appearance of the spiral? Does it shrink or expand?

Quickly look up and stare at someone's face. What do you see? How might reversing the spin affect the illusion? Make a guess. Then, try it and find out.

What Happened?

The twisting movement of the spiral made the pattern appear as if it was expanding or contracting. To help maintain the same appearance, your brain kept on adjusting what you saw. When you looked away, your brain kept on "adjusting" and produced an illusion of changing size.

DOUBLE SPIN

Use this spiral within a spiral pattern to construct another spinner. What happens to this pattern as it turns?

SPIRALING SPIRE

Here's an offset spiral pattern that produces the illusion of 3D. But wait, it's even weirder. Slowly spin the page and illusion of depth becomes greater!

Lengthy Confusion

There are dozens of illusions that fool your brain into seeing lengths that are different from what they actually are! These illusions use all sorts of "tricks" to produce their distorting effect. Some illusions use background patterns. Others are based upon relative positions. Still others, set up false comparisons with neighboring objects. But even though the tactics are different, the results are the same.

Take a look at the red and blue lines. Is the red line longer than the blue? If so, by how much?

A Little Background

As you may have guessed (after all, this is a book about optical illusions), the blue line and red line are the exact same length. Go ahead, use a ruler and compare their lengths. Amazing!

The background lines contain simple cues that remind your brain of a three-dimensional scene. By accepting a little "depth," your visual processing gets tricked. It assumes that the blue line is a little closer to you. Once that assumption is set, the illusion begins. Your brain does an automatic adjustment to the scene and shrinks the blue line. At the same time, it stretches the "more distant" red line, making it appear longer.

TICKET TO TRICKERY
Don't forget your ticket! It's your entrance into this incredible universe of optical illusions. It's also a great visual trick. Take a look. Although they don't appear it, the red and blue lines are the exact same length.

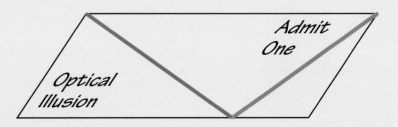

3D Foolery
This is another length illusion that uses a false sense of 3D. Unlike the previous illusion, this background appears tilted. Both the outline and the writing suggest that the image is a rectangle that is leaning back. Your brain accepts the suggestion and adds a little bit of 3D processing.

It's this extra brainwork that throws things off. When the ticket is assumed to have some depth, the apparent line lengths are "altered" to fit the misconception. No problem. The red line gets lengthened. The blue line gets shortened.

WHICH LINE IS LONGER?

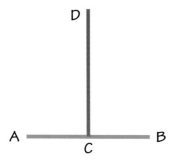

Inquiring Minds

Most people will agree that line CD looks longer than line AB. The key word here is "looks." Both AB and CD are the exact same length. But what makes them appear different? For a moment, let's investigate this as a scientist might by examining and testing three possible reasons for this illusion.

1. The printed letters break up the space and create the length distortion. Okay, so if the printed letters caused the illusion, let's get rid of them. Does the illusion still work?

You bet it does, so we can scratch the print theory.

2. At one time, it was thought that your eyes tired more easily from looking at vertical lines than at horizontal lines. This eye fatigue was believed to create this illusion. Let's test this theory by turning the illusion on its side. Does the trickery still work?

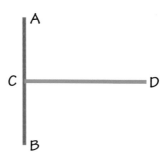

For most people, it seems to. Even though the lines switched positions, CD still appears slightly longer.

3. A more modern theory suggests that things look longer when they are whole. Lines that are broken into smaller pieces appear smaller. We can test this theory by moving the lines so that when they cross, they form equal parts. Does the illusion still work?

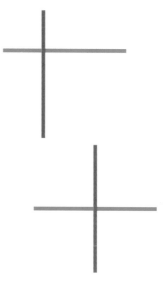

Not anymore. This theory apparently makes the most sense for explaining this illusion. However, things change! Scientists are always learning new things. From new knowledge, new ideas arise. Perhaps you'll be the scientist who develops a better theory of this illusion!

ON THE SIDE

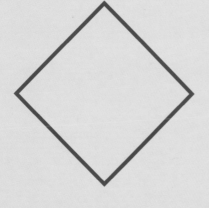

Although they may not look it, both squares are the exact same size. Your brain gets tricked into "seeing" the diamond as a slightly larger figure.

Lengthy Lines

It's quiz time! Match up these lines into pairs of equal lengths.

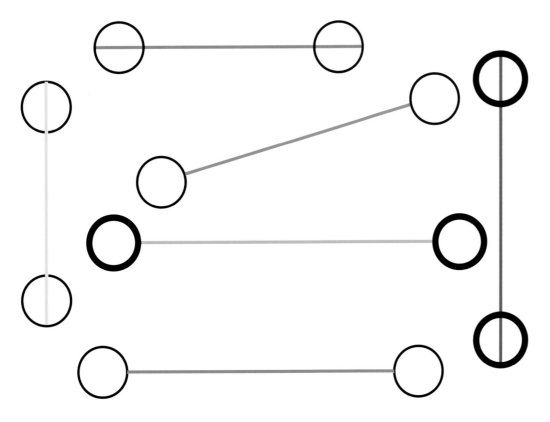

Answer: Red and blue, green and yellow, purple and orange.

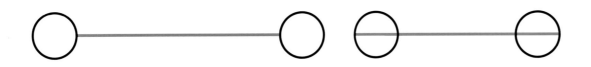

How Come?

This powerful illusion is created by two visual tricks that work together. One trick is the interruption of straight lines. When a circle crosses over a line, it cuts it into smaller segments. You are more likely to see a line separated into pieces as shorter in length than an intact line. The other trick has to do with the overall appearance of the line. When the circles were tacked onto the end points of the line, they made the line seem longer.

Even when the lines are placed side-by-side, the illusion produces a strong distortion. Go ahead. Use a ruler. The red lines are the exact same length.

IT'S RELATIVE Suppose you wanted to look taller. Would you stand next to people who were shorter, taller, or of the same height? Most of us would pick shorter people. By standing next to people who are not as tall, your height would help you "stand out" from the crowd. Can you apply this tactic to the next illusion?

Which center circle looks bigger?

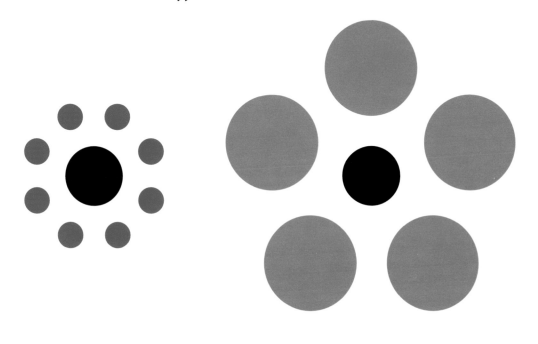

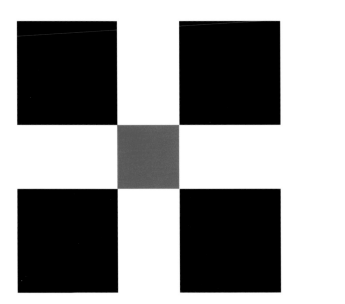

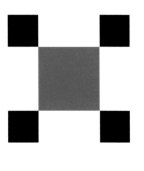

Compare, Compare, Compare

Both center circles are the same size, although the one surrounded by blue dots appears bigger. Your brain is constantly comparing things. It was tricked into thinking that the center circle on the left was big because it was larger than the surrounding objects. At the same time, it was tricked into thinking that the center circle on the right was small, since it appeared smaller than its surrounding objects. Your brain used this concept to create an unfair comparison between equal-sized circles.

COMPARE AGAIN

Which middle square is larger? Once more, the comparison concept is at work. The square surrounded by the larger blocks doesn't look as big as the same-sized square surrounded by smaller blocks.

Shape Illusions

Examine the square on the left. It looks like a traditional square. All four sides are formed by straight lines. All four corners are right angles. Face it. This square is a square.

Look at the pattern below the square. Nothing much going on here either. Four sets of half circle designs. That's what they are.

The illusion occurs when we place that same square over the loop design.

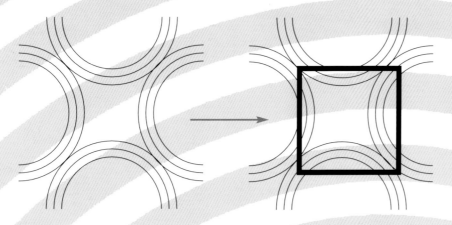

What Happened? The square appears to bulge. I said "appears" because, believe it or not, the square hasn't changed at all. This illusion is so strong that you may want to check it out with a straight edge. The sides remain perfectly straight! Their curved appearance is an illusion. The loops created misleading cues that tricked your brain into seeing something that wasn't there.

IN A PINCH A square placed inside a circle can distort the circle's smooth curve. Does the circle appear to be "pinched in" at each corner of the square?

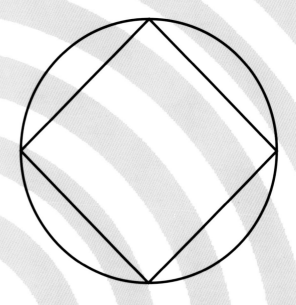

SQUISH SQUASH

The inner circle is perfectly round. The spokes, however, create the illusion of a somewhat squished shape.

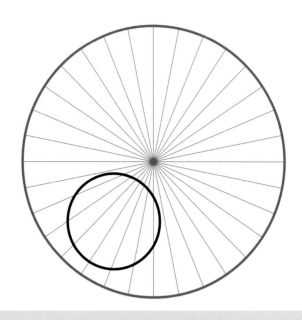

MORE DISTORTIONS

These distortions can also be created without curves. Take a look at the figures on the left. The closer you come to these shapes, the more distorted they appear. But as you probably guessed, their "warped" look is only an illusion.

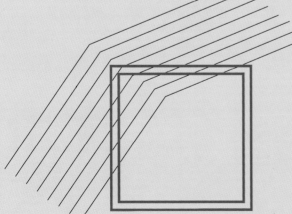

31

Slants

How would you describe the letters that compose the word on the right? Are they printed vertically straight or do they have a slight tilt? Do they all lean in the same direction? How positive are you?

A Better View

Hold this page at arm's length. Squint down your eyes. Examine the letters again. What happens to the slant as you shut down your eyes?

When you squinted, you lost some of the image information. Instead of seeing individual blocks of color, these shapes blurred together and formed the outline of a straight line! The tilted appearance of the whole letter is an illusion. It is created by the offset in the colored blocks. When you couldn't see the distinct pattern of these blocks, the illusion disappeared!

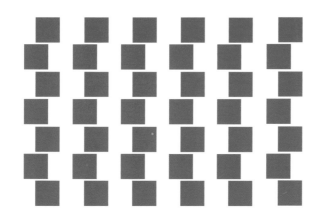

LEANING LAYERS? Does the pattern look warped?

You bet it does! It's an illusion that is suggested by the offset of the blocks. The slight shift tricks your brain into "seeing" slanted layers. But do any of these slants exist? Only in your mind. Place the straight edge of a ruler beneath each line and you'll observe the perfectly straight and flat arrangement.

SEPARATED AT BIRTH?

Here's a "double" illusion that you'll want to check with a ruler. First off, the two blue lines are perfectly horizontal. They remain parallel even through they look as if they widen as you go to the right.

This second part is even stranger. The red lines continue straight across the blue horizontal lines. That's right. The red lines aren't offset. Check them with a ruler. Amazing!

Here's another example:

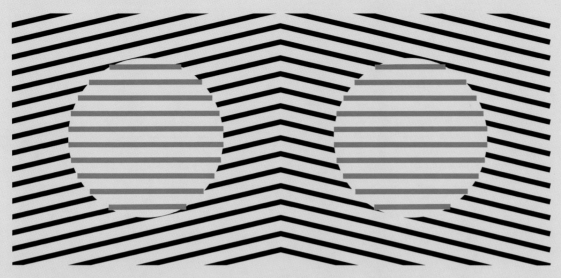

Cool shades, huh? The lines in the circles are perfectly horizontal. It's the background pattern that suggests their tilt. Always open to suggestion, your brain makes a "wrong turn" and sees something different from what it actually is!

PERPLEXING PARALLEL PATTERNS

By themselves, the seven lines below seem perfectly parallel. No problem in seeing that. However, look what happens when you add a confusing pattern. The lines take on a new "leaning." Although the tilt may be new, the illusion isn't. It's based upon the Zollner illusion, which was first published in 1860.

Do these green lines appear to separate or come together?

How about now?

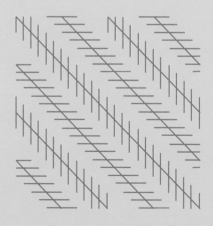

Patterns

Organize, organize, organize. Take a look at these two patterns of shapes. Which pattern seems to be composed of vertical columns? Which pattern seems to contain horizontal rows?

How about this one? Columns or rows?

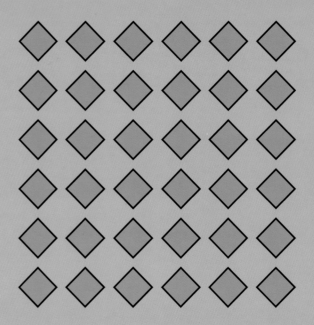

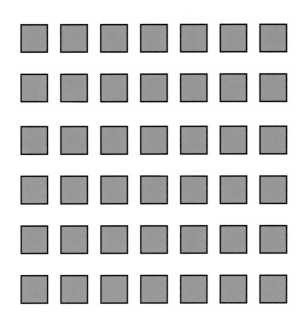

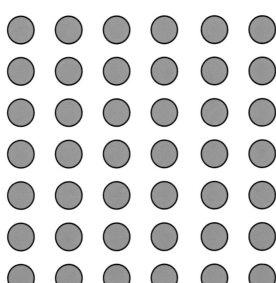

As you may have figured out, the spacing between objects determines how you organize the pattern. In the first pattern, the objects were more closely spaced along each of the horizontal rows. Your brain used this cue to construct a pattern of horizontal rows. In the second pattern, the objects were more closely spaced in vertical columns. Here, your brain constructed a pattern of vertical columns. The third pattern was formed by objects that were equally spaced in all directions. That's why the pattern flipped back and forth between columns and rows.

TRYING TIRING TRIANGLES

Stare at this pattern of triangles for several seconds. Soon, your brain will begin organizing these triangles into all sorts of imaginary patterns, shapes, peaks, and shades.

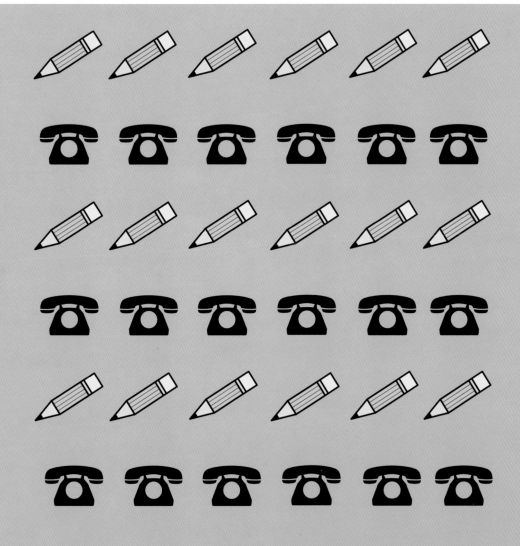

NAME THAT PATTERN

What is the first pattern you see when you look at the grid of objects on the left? Most people will see alternating rows of pencils and telephones. Even though the grid can also be broken into vertical columns of alternating objects, most people don't see it. It's easier to group similar things together.

Which side of the rectangle below is darker? Are you sure? Good. Now take a pencil and place it along the border, dividing the block in half. Now, which side is darker? Remove the pencil. What happens now?

COOL SHADES

place pencil here

What Happened?

It's the special shading of these adjacent blocks that creates this powerful illusion. Both halves are identical. However, they are not filled with a single shade of gray. Each half contains a gradual change from light gray to dark gray. This type of change is called a gradient.

The dividing line forms where the dark border of the left half meets the light border of the right half. When this margin is uncovered, you can easily detect the difference in shades. However, when it gets covered by the pencil, your brain gets confused. It can't detect a distinct edge and mistakenly assumes that each block is filled with its own uniform shade of gray.

NO WAY! The two ovals are exactly the same shade (actually both are filled with the identical shade). When placed over different background shades, one oval appears lighter than the other.

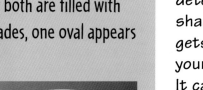

LET IT BLEED
Hold this page at arm's length. Can the square on the right fit between the other two squares? To test your guess (and save this illusion for the next person), use a ruler.

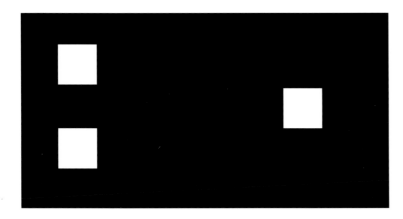

COMPARED TO WHAT?
Our sense of shade and color depends upon how an object appears against a background. Examine the two inner squares below. Although they don't look it, both squares are the exact same shade of gray. The square on the left is placed over a light background and appears dark. The square on the right is placed over a dark background. In contrast, it appears light.

This illusion is caused by the brightness of a reflected image. The black background reflects relatively little light. The white squares, however, reflect a great deal of light. When the bright light falls upon the retina, its effect spreads beyond the focused image. It excites neighboring cells to produce an "expanded" response. This extra response suggests that the square is bigger than it actually is.

SHADY COMPARISON
Look at the purple bar that stretches across the two colored boxes. It contains a uniform shade of purple. There's no trick going on—not yet anyway.

Now, place your finger across the bar so that the whole illustration is separated into a right and left half. Does the purple appear the same on both sides of your finger?

What Happened?
The purple that is surrounded by the blue appears slightly brighter than the purple that remains against the pink background. This illusion is based upon a comparison of an object to its background. In this case, your brain was tricked into mistakenly "tweaking" the bar colors.

Remove your finger and examine the bar again. Once more, the bar appears to be filled with a single color. Without a finger forming a "distinct border," your brain finds it more difficult to assign two different shades to the bar.

37

Afterimages

Stare at the center of this bull's-eye. Slowly count to ten.

Try not to move. Keep your focus on the center dot.

Now quickly switch your focus to the triangle. What do you see?

The ghost-like image that appears at the triangle is called an *afterimage*. Compare the afterimage to the original bull's eye. How are they alike? How are they different?

What's the Scoop?

Afterimages are illusions that appear after your vision has been overstimulated. Over-stimulation can be caused by a camera's bright flash—those floating spots are afterimages! After-images can also be caused by staring at the same thing for a long period of time.

As you look at an object, the light that falls on your retina alters the chemistry balance of your eye. This change temporarily "imprints" a kind of image on your retina. When you look away from the object, you see its afterimage illusion. Although it's the same size and shape, it "materializes" in opposite shades (like a black-and-white photographic negative).

COOL CAT Let the cool cat go out on a limb. Stare at its white nose for 15 seconds. Then, shift your vision to the circle. Keep looking and within a few seconds your feline friend will appear out of thin air.

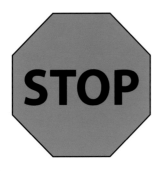

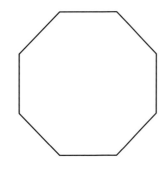

SEEING RED? Stare at the center of the stop sign on the left for 15 seconds. Switch your focus to the center of the blank outline to the right. Does anything appear?

KING OF ILLUSIONS

Stare at the dot in the center of the picture below for 20 seconds. Quickly switch your focus to the star in the center of the newspaper cover to the right. Who appears?

GRAND OLD FLAG

Stare at the center of this odd-colored flag for 15 seconds. Switch your focus to a white wall or ceiling. Does anything more American materialize?

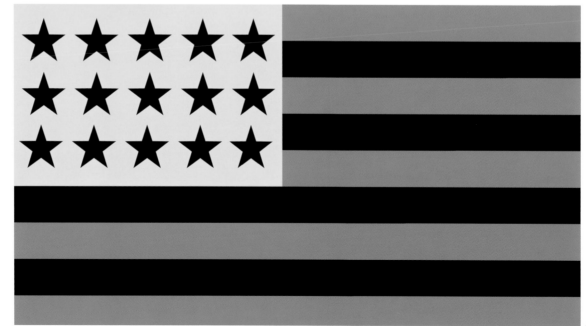

The Daily Tabloid

THE KING SEEN EVERYWHERE!

★

Image Stretch

Do you like secret codes? If so, can you figure out what this code on the right says?

THINK ABOUT IT

Have you ever seen a stretched sign painted on a roadway? Here's one of a bicycle that's been painted on a bike path. Why do you think this image is distorted?

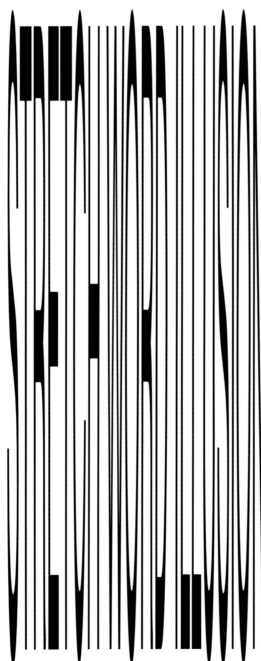

In order to decode this message, hold the bottom edge of the book at eye level. Look across the page. The letters appear to shrink down, making them easy to read.

You Can Do It Too!

Although you can make stretched images by hand, its fast and easy to create them with a computer. All you need is a graphics program and a printer. Draw an image or enter a word. Highlight this area. Use the "stretch" command to distort the image. When the word has been stretched beyond recognition, print it out. Challenge friends and family members to uncover the decoding secret!

Examine these photos. As you've probably guessed, they were all stretched by computer. Can you identify each subject without viewing the image from its edge?

Mosaics

What is this image on the right? After you've made your guess, look at it from across the room. What happens to its blocky appearance?

At a distance, the image takes shape. It's like the saying "seeing the forest through the trees." Up close, the individual squares command your attention. You see sharp-edged blocks filled with different colors.

When the image is held at a distance, things begin to blur. No longer do you see the sharp edges, but instead the blocks begin to "work" with each other. Your brain processes the similarities and begins to form an image. Searching its visual memories, it uncovers subjects that resemble the layout of blurring boxes. When enough information has been decoded, your brain sees a familiar subject in this blocky mess.

IMPRESS YOUR FRIENDS!

You can make a mosaic block just like this one. All you need is access to a computer graphics program, a photo, and a scanner. Scan your picture (or take a new one with a digital camera). Open the picture in a graphics program. Highlight any region of the picture you want to use (or select the whole picture). Then apply a mosaic block effect. You should be able to access controls that determine the size of the blocks. Apply the effect and your computer does the rest.

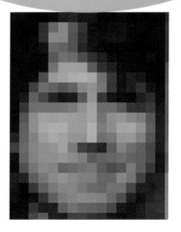

Now that you know about mosaics, what is it?

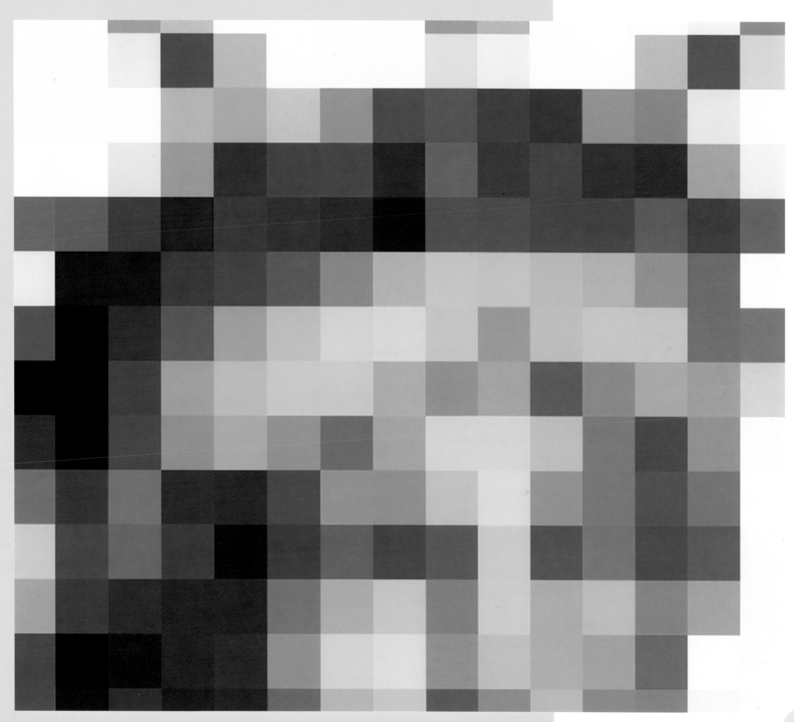

Illusionary Figures

Do you see the black triangle below? Great. Which way is it pointing? Is it brighter or darker than its background? Are the sides of the triangle straight or wavy?

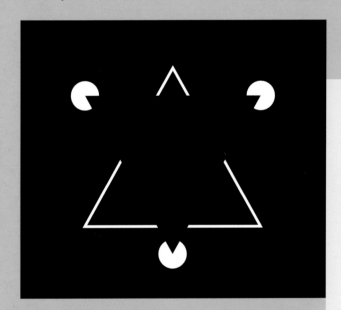

Most likely you "saw" a black triangle that faced downwards. It was slightly darker than the background. All three sides were formed by straight lines. Right? The only trouble is, the triangle does not exist! Let me repeat that statement: *There is no triangle.*

Your brain made it up. It was fooled. But it wasn't entirely your brain's fault. The image had clues that led you into taking the wrong shortcuts.

When an object overlaps another object, it can cover up some of the lower shape. In this illusion, it appeared as if something was blocking out parts of a triangle outline and three circles. The most logical (and simplest) shape that could accomplish this "cover-up" was a triangle. Hence, your brain built an illusionary triangle to help make sense of the "incomplete" pattern.

Above is a set of misleading cues that create several whiter-than-white circles. Like the illusionary triangle, this pattern only exists in your mind.

In the illusion below, do you "see" the white circles at each of the grid intersections? Too bad. Like the triangle, they exist only in your mind!

And to conclude this section, here are a pine tree, a TV screen, a pentagon, and a circle—none of which exist.

45

More Things That Don't Exist

Look into this pattern of spheres. Can you find the imaginary cube?

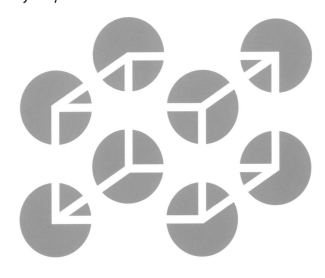

How about a four-sided pyramid?

LET THE SUNSHINE
Take a look at the illusion below. Do you see a Sun-like circle at the center of these lines? Good. Remember it, because it's not there!

Prove It Isn't So
Get two rulers. Place them on either side of any of the lines that cuts across this image. The line should be isolated (but not covered). Follow it from one end to the other. Can you still see the curved edge of the Sun? What happened to it?

Your brain constructed the circle. It was tricked by the fading color pattern that "suggested" a printed shape. This suggestion was so strong that your brain constructed an illusion to make the image fit in with your experiences.

SEEING THROUGH THE TRICKERY

There are three shapes below. The outer shapes are two slightly eclipsed moons. The inner shape looks like a convex lens. Easy.

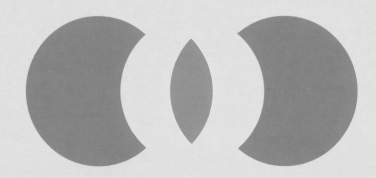

When we slide these shapes together, your brain creates an imaginary scene. No longer do you see three separate and distinct pieces. Instead, the shapes and shades work together to produce an illusion of two overlapping circles.

SCREEN PLAY
Do you see the circle in the middle of the grid below? As you probably guessed, this too is an illusion. This is no circle. Your brain created this shape from the offset of lines. Instead of seeing a grid with misplaced lines, your brain organized the scene into a circle cut from a background pattern.

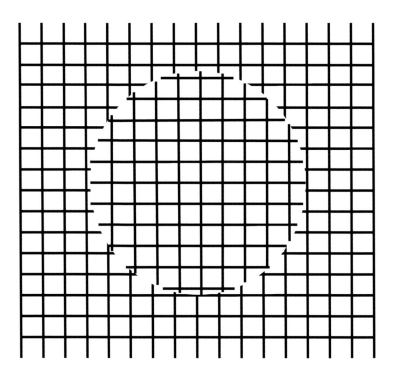

ON THE EDGE
Nice curve. But, like the previous circle, it doesn't exist. Use a hand lens and you'll see that no line forms this illusionary edge.

POWERFUL PATTERNS

Stare into this set of circles. Do you see any spokes that project from the center of this design? What color are they? Are they stationary or do they seem to race around the image?

No one knows for certain why these color spokes appear. One theory is based upon your rapid eye movements. As you look at this image, your eyes dart back and forth faster and faster. The changing view creates a continuous stream of visual messages. At a certain rate, these messages may resemble the brain's code for colors.

These wavy lines suggest a powerful 3D image of hills and valleys.

KIDS IN THE HALL

Compare the size of these three kids. Although they don't appear it, all three are the exact same size! That's because the pattern that fills this hallway produces a powerful trick. Here's how it works.

You "know" this drawing is flat. However, the grid pattern "suggests" three-dimensional qualities. This suggestion is so strong that it confuses your brain!

Since your brain sees this hallway with some three dimensional qualities, it begins to tweak the image. The result of the "tweaking" is a size misconception. The kid up front appeared smaller while the kid at the back of the hall was stretched.

HAIR-RAISING EXPERIENCE

Here's a weird pattern. To observe the effect, you'll need to place the page at eye level. Move the book so that your eye is positioned at the point where all these lines seem to come together (several inches from the bottom right corner).

Close one eye. Look at the image. Can you see how the lines pop up like the bristles of a hairbrush?

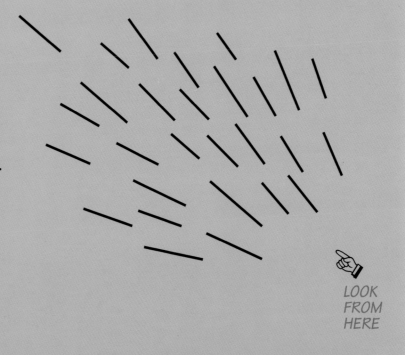

LOOK FROM HERE

49

Broken Lines

Compare the two angles below. The green lines appear solid. Those that form the red angle, however, appear to "pinch" and shift slightly wherever they cross the horizontal lines. Look closely and you'll see that the red lines don't break. They remain solid. It's an illusion that occurs when lines intersect at slight angles.

The two vertical lines seem to offset the edges of this perfect square.

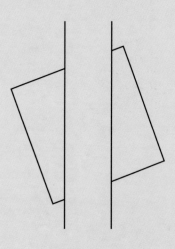

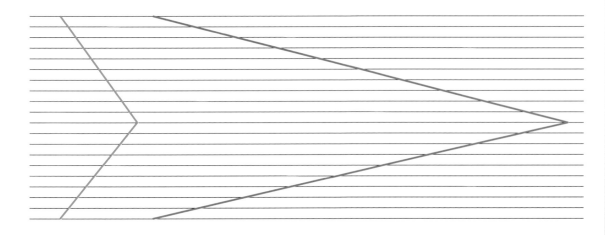

Which line meets up with line A?

Line C. Interrupted lines are tricky things to follow. Your vision is easily distracted from a "straight" path and incorrectly "sees" line A connecting to the uppermost of the three choices.

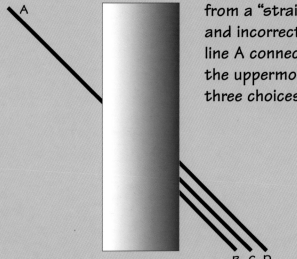

Is line AB continuous or does its middle section "move up" slightly? Make a guess, and then use a ruler to find out.

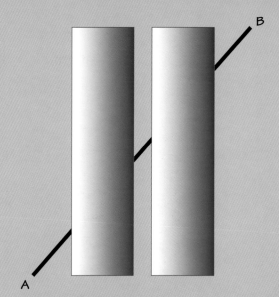

IMAGINARY INTERFERENCE

You don't even need a real object to produce a broken line illusion. An illusionary rectangle is strong enough to create the same "shifty" effect.

THROWING CURVES

This type of illusion is even more confusing when the lines are curved. Suppose you extended the two upper arcs below the parallel lines. To most people, it appears as if the extended sections would fit in *between* the lower portion arcs. Not so. The upper arc is continuous with the lower inner arc.

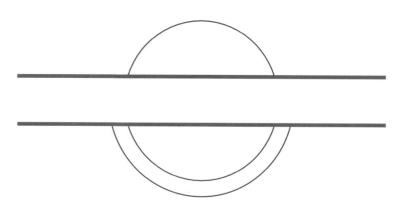

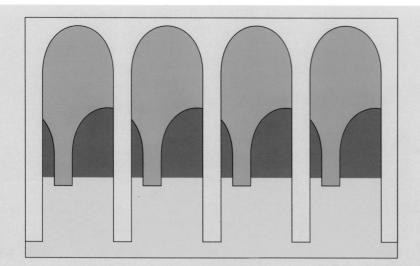

NICE ARCH

Although they don't appear it, all of the arches in this drawing meet up perfectly. It's the broken lines that create the illusion.

CASE CLOSED

It's the letter "F"–or is it? Your brain seems to think so. Although these lines don't complete the "F," they strongly suggest the letter. Your brain likes to see familiar things. When it is presented with this open figure, it closes it into something it recognizes: an embossed "F." Case closed.

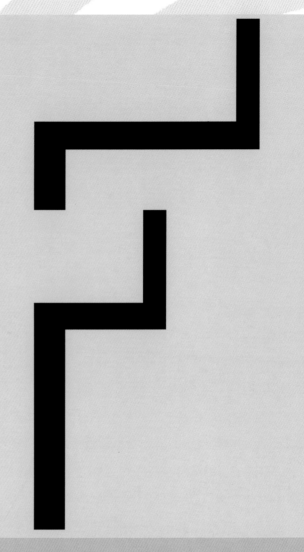

Like the "F," this pattern can also be closed by seeing it in 3D. Once the image clicks from arrowheads to cubes, it takes on a whole new meaning: a row of five boxes.

QUIZ TIME

Can you construct a whole object from seeing just a few parts? Here's your chance to find out. How many of the following images can you identify?

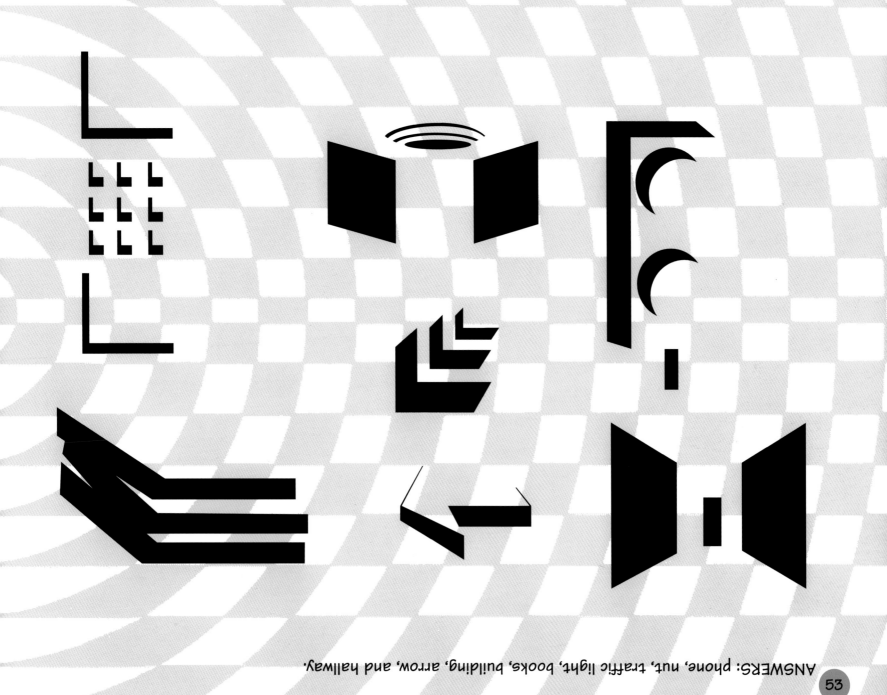

Flip-Flopping Faces

Here's a familiar illusion. It's based upon a drawing that was first published in 1915! Can you see why it was originally called "My Wife and My Mother-in-law"?

This type of illusion is called an ambiguous figure. Its meaning is not fixed. Instead, it depends upon the way you interpret it. This figure flip-flops between the portrait of a young woman and that of an older woman. Can you see both people? Which one did you see first?

The Younger Woman
The younger woman's face is turned away from you. She is looking to the back over her right shoulder. The horizontal red line forms her necklace. You can see her nose, eyelashes, and chin in profile.

The Older Woman
The older woman looks down with her chin pressed against her chest. The horizontal red line forms her lips. Her nose has a small wart.

54

A RABBIT OR DUCK?

This illusion was created around the turn of the century. Its appearance flip-flops between two popular animals.

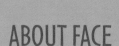

THINK ABOUT IT

Does your previous experience affect what you see? You bet it does! If people are shown pictures of rabbits before seeing this illusion, they are more likely to see a rabbit. If, however, they are shown pictures of ducks, they are more likely to see a duck.

ABOUT FACE

Here's another flip-flopping mind boggler that appeared around the turn of the century. Can you see the profile of the Native American chief? Keep looking at this face and it will soon transform into an Inuit turned in the direction of his igloo. Can you "see" both images at the same time?

More Flip-Flops

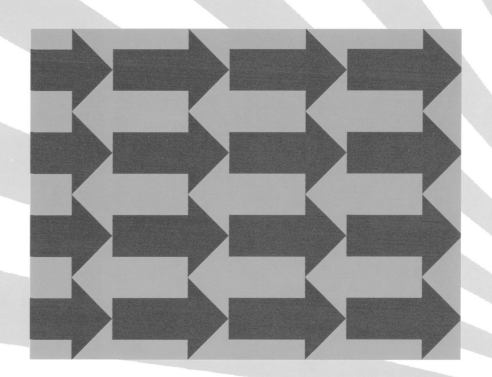

Quickly flash your gaze to the pattern on the right. Then look back up here and answer these three questions. What do you see? What color were the objects? Which way did they point?

Get the Point?

Most people first see a pattern of red arrows pointing to the right. If they continue to examine the image, another pattern appears: green arrows pointing to the left.

Why are the red arrows most often seen first? Some people believe that we have learned to associate red with danger and importance. Therefore, our brain is "pre-set" to look for things that are red.

ANOTHER SIGN

Suppose you were driving down the road and stopped at an intersection. You look up and see this sign. What does it mean?

Most people interpret this sign as four yellow arrows. The arrows appear to indicate four directions. But can you see anything else?

A few people won't see the arrows first. Instead, they see a black "H" printed over a yellow diamond. Can you make this image flip-flop between these two views?

VASE

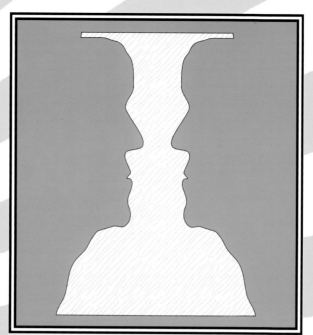

Here's another illusion that you've probably seen before. It's an ambiguous figure that flip-flops between two profiles and a vase.

PUZZLING PATTERN

Stare at the center of this pattern as you count to five S-L-O-W-L-Y. What happens? Flip-flopping madness! Does the pattern remain stable or does it appear to shift?

So far our ambiguous figures have flip-flopped in two dimensions. But did you know that this type of illusion can also jump out in 3D?

Look at the drawing below. What do you see? Keep looking. Does the outline remain flat or does it appear to take on some depth?

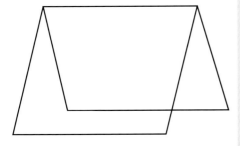

Most likely, your brain has added 3D to this flat drawing. Instead of accepting it as a 2D pattern, your brain has organized the lines into something with depth. From experience, you've learned that this arrangement strongly resembles a bent rectangle. This memory is so strong that it can be used to "build" a 3D object. Instead of remaining flat, the lines construct the appearance of an open greeting card.

Page Poppers

RIGHT OR LEFT

When you added 3D to the image, you had the choice of opening the "greeting card" to the right or to the left. Which way did you first see it? Did the closer edge bend slightly downwards to the left or upwards to the right? The drawings below show the two possible views. Practice flipping the lines between these two appearances. Although it may be difficult at first, it gets easier with practice.

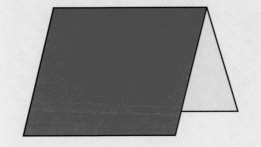

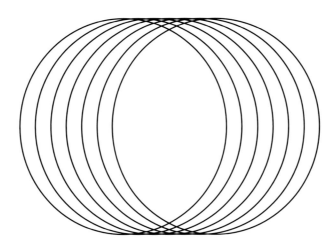

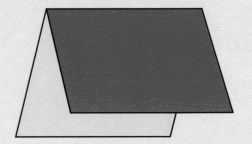

The set of circles at the left can take on a 3D effect and appear like a coil. Do you see it? Great. Can you make the coil "pop" from right to left?

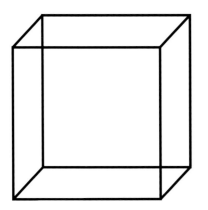 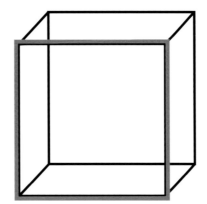 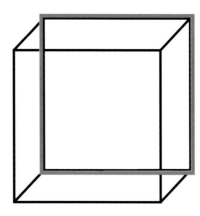

REVERSING CUBE

Take a look at the outline above. Can you see why it's called a "reversing cube"? Like the greeting card, this cube has two logical appearances. There is no reason that one should make more sense than the other. So when you look at it, you'll see a cube with its nearest side (outlined in red) facing downwards to the left or upwards to the right.

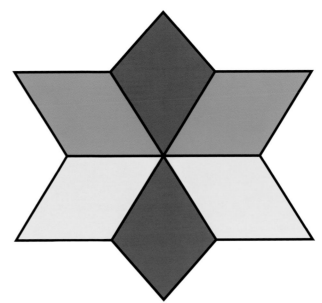

Can you make the shape above jump between the three forms shown at the right? Can you uncover other ways to "see" this figure with depth?

A New Outlook

The staircase on the right presents little room for doubt. The four steps rise from right to left. However, it can have another appearance. Can you see this image as an overhang? Most likely not. However, help is on the way. Read the HINT below.

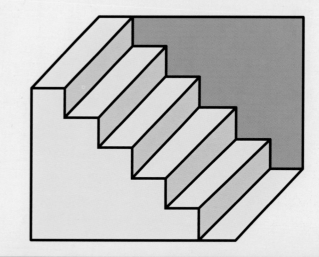

HINT

To uncover the overhang, turn the page upside down. Once this new staircase "materializes," slowly rotate the page back to its upright position. This technique can help produce the overhang. Don't give up. It will take some practice to keep the overhang from "flipping" back to steps.

THICK AS A BRICK

Most likely you saw the drawing on the right as a pattern of bricks tilting down from the top right corner. The bright surfaces are the brick tops. But would you believe that the surfaces can flip from side to side? It's not easy to do. To help change your outlook on this image, rotate the page upside down. The brick pattern should "flip." Try to maintain this pattern as you rotate the page back around. It's difficult, but it can be done.

HEX MAKES THE SPOT

Stare at the center of the hexagon pattern. What happens?

Within a few moments, your brain probably got tired of seeing a flat target. To "liven" things up, it built something with a little more depth: a cube. But which cube did it construct? Like the coil on page 58, the near side of this object can face right or left. Can you isolate both views of the cube? How quickly can you flip the hexagon image between the two cube views?

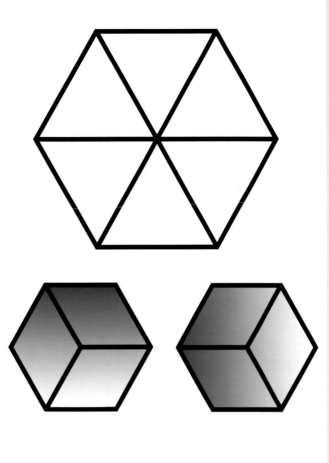

MIXED-UP FOLD (THE 3D TARGET)

Make a 3D model of this illusion. Fold a sheet of paper in half lengthwise. Set it upright on edge. Close one eye and keep looking at the crease line. What happens? Can you get the image to switch from an open book to a peaked roof? Keep trying.

MIXED-UP FOLD (THE 2D TARGET)

Stare at the lines. As you can see, this image becomes 3D. Keep staring and the direction of the bend will switch every few seconds.

IMPOSSIBLE FIGURES

Have you ever seen something that looked impossible to build? Totally impossible? As impossible as the thingamajig on the right?

Does this thingamajig have two or three prongs? It depends upon which way you look at it. Start out from the right end and it has two prongs. Look at it from the other end and it has three prongs. Weird? Very. Impossible? Definitely.

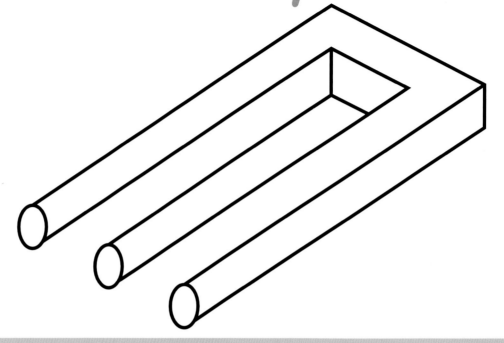

THE SCIENCE OF IMPOSSIBILITY

We live in a universe of 3D space. All objects—from televisions to professional wrestlers—have height, length, and width.

A picture (or photo or image or painting...) is a flat representation of a 3D scene or object. Because the image is flat, it doesn't have to conform to the laws of 3D space. In other words, you can cheat. You can draw objects that distort, twist, and destroy the concepts of three dimensions.

Take a look at the postage stamps on the left. They were issued in Sweden in 1982. All of them are real stamps with unreal objects.

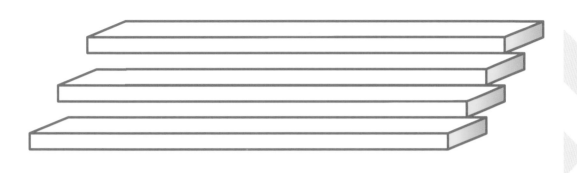

Many impossible figures can also be viewed as unstable illusions. As you stare at them, you'll find that their appearance flip-flops between two logical looks. Which one is correct? It depends. How many boards make up the stack on the left?

FLIP-FLOPPING AWAY

Try building these crazy crates and you'll find yourself boxed in by the laws of physics. You'll also experience how figures that are impossible can shift quickly between their unstable forms.

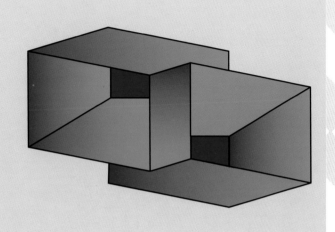

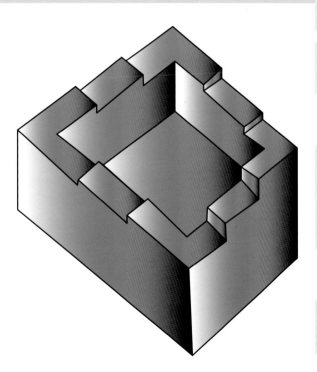

Here's a basic impossible staircase. What happens when you go up or down these stairs?

More Impossibilities

Now, it's time to extend impossibilities into the universe of 3D. Photocopy this page onto a sheet of stiff paper. Cut out the two sides of the window. Tape them together and trim away the excess paper. Attach a 1-foot-long dental floss to the X. Make about twenty turns in the floss. Hold the window about 1 foot away at eye level. Release the window and observe its spin. What do you see? Does the window appear to turn in a circle or does it look as if it flips back and forth?

The weird effect was explored almost a half century ago by the psychologist Adelbert Ames. He's the same guy who first constructed the distorted room in which a person appears to shrink as they cross from one side of the room to the other.

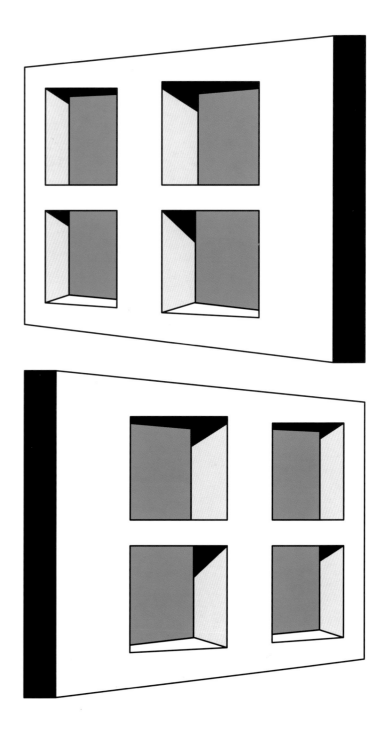

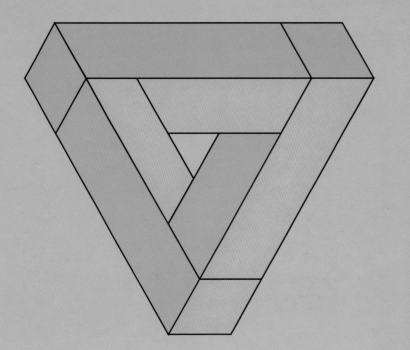

IMPOSSIBLE POSSIBILITIES

On the left is a drawing of an impossible triangle. As you can see, the twists of its frame can only exist on paper. Obviously, there is no way that a triangle like this can exist as an real object–or can it?

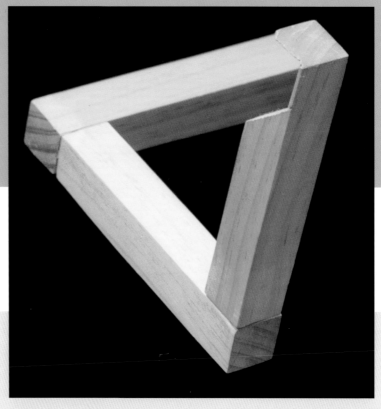

Hang on to your brains. Here's an actual and unretouched photograph of an impossible triangle! What? How can this wooden frame have impossible twists? What's going on here?

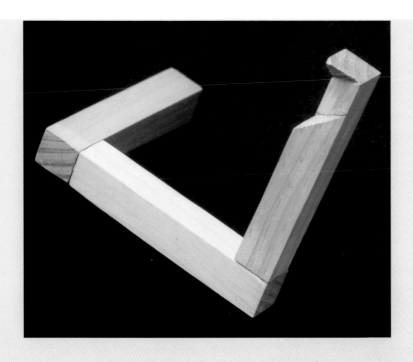

Trickery

This is a real visual trick. What appears to be a closed triangle isn't. The wooden frame is bent and open. From the camera's view, however, the open ends overlap, making it appear to be a closed triangle. If we change our view, we can see what this tricky frame really looks like.

65

Get two pennies and stack them between the thumb of one hand and the index finger of the other. Quickly move these fingers back and forth so that the coins rub against each other. How many coins do you see?

Staying Power

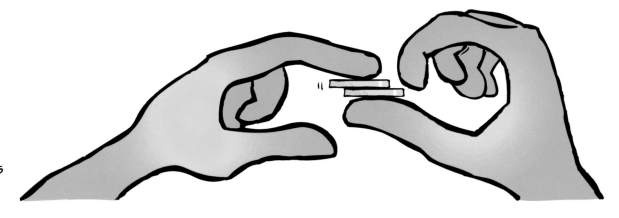

Extra Cash

The "extra" coin that appeared in the stack was an illusion. This illusion is based upon something called "persistence of vision." This term is used to describe the lingering of an image. Even though an object may disappear, its image lingers on for a fraction of a second. Because the coins moved quickly back and forth, they created a persistent image that appeared like a third coin.

HANGING AROUND   Around 1825, a new "toy" was created. It was called a thaumatrope, which is a fancy word meaning "turning marvel." This toy used the persistence of vision to blend two images into one.

Take a look at the poor fish below. It's out of its element. However, with the help of a modern thaumatrope, we'll place it back in a bowl of water!

PENCIL FLIPPER

A pencil flipper is a simple device that uses the persistence of vision to blend two images into one. To build this flipper, make a copy of any of the image pairs shown on pages 66 and 67. Fold the pair along the dotted line and tape the edge together. Slip this frame over the end of a pencil. Use tape along the upper and lower border to secure the images to the pencil.

Place the pencil between your palms. Quickly roll your hands back and forth.

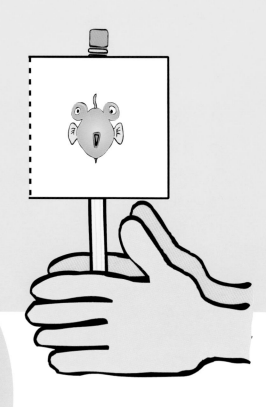

YOUR TURN

Think of a cool scene made up of two distinct things. Draw one object on one side of a pencil flipper frame. Draw the other object on the opposite side. Construct the flipper and use it to put the image back together.

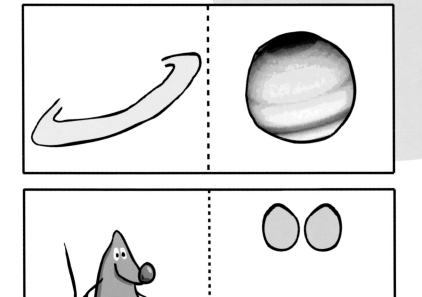

CONSTRUCTING HISTORY

The first thaumatropes didn't use pencils. Instead, they were constructed from a two-sided disk that was taped to a piece of string. When the string was rolled, the disk spun. Pictures drawn on both sides of this disk blended into a single image. Do you think you can make the device from this description? Give it a try.

Deep Thoughts

Shut one eye. Look around the room. Does the room appear flat or does it still have depth? To most of us, the room still appears 3D. Even though your view may be limited to one eye, there is still plenty of information to construct depth.

CUES, CUES, EVERYWHERE A CUE Take a look at the two playing cards below. Most of use have no trouble in constructing the original scene. When this picture was taken, the king was in front of the four of clubs. It makes sense. All of the cues support this. Too bad all of the cues are misleading!

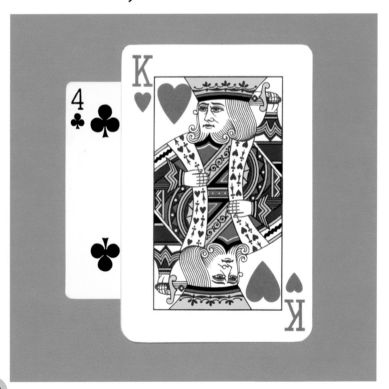

Overlap

Perhaps the strongest cue that suggests this illusion is the overlap of cards. Since the 4 of clubs appears partially hidden by the king, it is logical to construct a scene in which the king is the front card.

Now for the illusion. The 4 of clubs is only a portion of a card. It has been trimmed into a shape that suggests it has been overlapped. Your brain does the rest. It assumes that this card has a complete shape. Since you couldn't see the whole card, your brain assumed that some of the shape was covered by the king.

Size

Another part of the illusion is size confusion. An object that is farther away appears smaller than a similar object that is nearby. The 4 and king were *never* the same size to begin with. The 4 was printed about two-thirds the size of the king. Your brain performed an automatic tweak and assumed that since the 4 of clubs looked slightly smaller, it had to be farther away.

Brightness

Brightness is another cue used to "see" a scene in 3D. Things that are closer to us often appear brighter. Since the 4 of clubs is printed slightly darker than the king, this cue also helps mislead your brain.

TRY IT YOURSELF To build this illusion you'll need a shoe box, pair of scissors, clay, and two playing cards. First, the cards. Ideally, cards from two different-sized decks work best. However, if you only have cards of one size, don't worry. You can still produce the effect. If they are old cards, you can trim off some of the outer white margin of one card, making it somewhat smaller. If you don't want to ruin a card, you can make a copy of the cards shown on the front page and paste it on a stiff paper support.

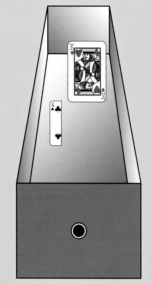

1. Cut a circular viewing hole in one end of a shoe box.

2. Cut off a 1-inch vertical strip from one end of the smaller card.

3. Use clay to position the cards in the box as shown here. Make sure that the smaller card is closer to the viewer and that the card edges align. The cards should be positioned so that the closer card appears slightly smaller than the more distant card.

4. Look through the viewing hole. What do you see?

INS AND OUTS OF SHADOWS Shadows are important clues for helping us construct depth. Sometimes they make a surface "pop" out. Other times, they make a surface appear to bend in. You can watch this reversing "pop" using a mask. Make sure that the mask is made of a hard material and that its inner surface has a 3D relief. Position the mask on a wall with the inner surface showing. Dim the lights. Stand about 10 feet away from the mask. Close one eye and look into the mask. Does the face go in or out? Move slowly to either side? Keep watching the mask and you may be surprised at the change you'll see!

Building 3D

Perhaps the strongest cues for building 3D are our separate right and left eye views. Any difference between these images gives information about distance. Objects that are farther have similar right and left eye views. The closer something gets, the more different the right and left eye views.

RIGHT EYED? LEFT EYED?
Are you right eyed or left eyed? Here's how you can find out. Shut one eye. Hold up a finger and look at a distant wall. Open the eye. Does the finger "jump" when you view it with two eyes? Now try the same trick with the other eye. Your dominant eye is the eye whose image keeps the finger in mostly the same place.

OLD-TIME TRICKS
As you've experienced, each eye has its own view (also called a vantage). If you are able to send a different vantage to each eye, you can create the illusion of 3D.

The images shown on these pages are called pseudomorphs. (pronounced su-doh-morfs). As you can see, each pseudomorph contains two images: a right eye and left eye view.

In order to see this 3D effect, you'll need to look at these images in a different and out-of-focus way. You'll need to relax your focus so that one image falls atop of the other. It's the same technique used to decode those "magic-image" stereograms.

Don't worry it you can't do this at first. It is a learned trick. Once you know how to do it, however, you'll be able to pop these images into 3D instantly!

OUT-OF-FOCUS PRACTICE
Here's a way to practice the technique. Hold this book about 1 foot away and look at the letters STEREO. Let your eyes relax so that they feel as if they are crossing. This sensation, sometimes called "lazy view," will give you a type of double vision. Keep looking with your lazy view at the S in STEREO. Try to relax enough so that the two S's come together and appear as a single letter. Take your time.

Once you can "fuse" the top letters, go down the list. Each pair of letters is a little more difficult to fuse. By the time you get to the O, you'll be well practiced in lazy-eye viewing and ready for quickly decoding pseudomorphs.

S S
T T
E E
R R
E E
O O

POP THESE IMAGES INTO 3D!
Hold this book about 1 foot away. Look at a pair of images. Relax.

Try to fuse the two images together. Relax.

In a few moments, the two images will overlap and its 3D look will emerge.

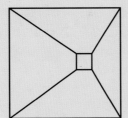
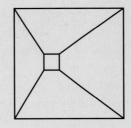
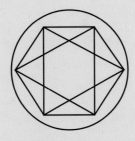
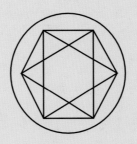

MORE CLUES
This effect can be made more intense by adding colors and shading. Look below. These "fills" help create the appearance of depth. They also suggest a fixed direction for the image "pop."

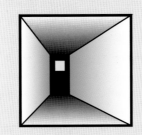
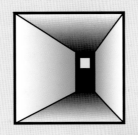

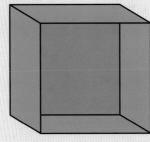
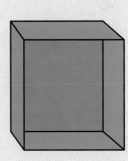

3-in-1?
Sometimes a third image is inserted between the pseudomorph pair. This image is just a copy of either the right or left image. Its central position, however, offers an easy target upon which to focus the 3D effect.

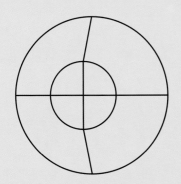
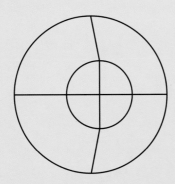
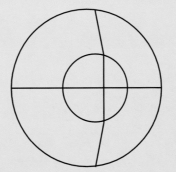

Popping Out of Paper

Take a look below. It's a pattern of Saturns. It gets better when you relax and view this pattern with the lazy view technique. As side-by-side planets fuse together, the image pops into 3D. This depth effect occurs because your brain assumes that a pair of side-by-side images is a single target. Therefore, it tries to correct it by "fusing" the two separate views into one.

Try It Yourself! It's really easy to make this type of false depth illusion. All you need are some identical coins, patience, and the ability to see the world with a "lazy view." On a sheet of white paper place a series of pennies in a straight row. The pennies should be separated by the length of another penny. Examine this pattern using the lazy-eye technique. Does the row take on a 3D appearance? Assemble a row of nickels beneath the pennies. Examine both patterns together. Does one row appear more forward than the other? How does the distance between pennies and nickels compare? Move the coins and experiment with different depths.

ORGANIZED RANDOMNESS Have you ever watched people stare into a colorful poster that illustrated some weird pattern? Suddenly, a smile bursts on their faces as they claim to see a starship beaming through space. Incredible? Yes. Contemporary? Somewhat. Although this type of illusion has become popular as a desktop computer trick, the basic principles have been around for years!

Random Dots Explained

The random dot stereogram, which many people call a magic-eye printout, has a right eye and left eye view. These views are broken up and printed as vertical strips. Look closely and you'll see how these strips alternate along the width of the poster. These columns produce a wavy effect.

The jumbled dots appear as a random pattern. I said "appear" because they are far from random. The side-by-side columns contain a special pattern of dots. This pattern is hidden in what looks like randomness. When overlapping the side-by-side columns, your brain identifies the similarities in dot pattern. These similarities identify a slightly different right and left eye view. Your brain fuses these views to produce an image that "jumps" out of the jumble!

Stereography

By the late 1800s, it was a living room rage. Everyone had to have one! This fad was a parlor toy that reproduced 3D views of the world. It was called a stereoscope.

The illusion of "depth" was created by viewing side-by-side images. Although the right- and left-hand photos may have looked identical, they weren't. The difference in the photos presented enough information to construct a 3D version of a flattened scene.

A stereoscope lens system was used to view and separate these side-by-side images. The right lens focused only on the right image. The left lens focused only on the left image. When these two separate images reached the brain, they were combined into a 3D view.

Build a 3D Stereoviewer

To build a viewer, all you need are two small and inexpensive hand lenses. The lenses should be identical and their surface free of scratches. The cheap plastic type that are often given away as party favors or packed beneath cereal boxes work fine!

Hold the hand lens between your thumb and index finger. Do the same with your other hand. Each lens should project outwards and remain horizontal. Hold the lenses over a stereophoto pair on the page. Adjust the lenses to a comfortable distance. If the photos are not in focus move the lenses closer or farther away from the desktop. Once they are in focus, keep looking. The magic will "jump out" at you!

Here are some side-by-side
stereophoto pairs.

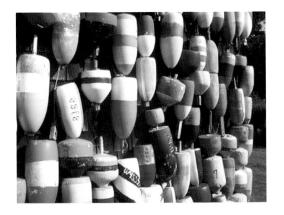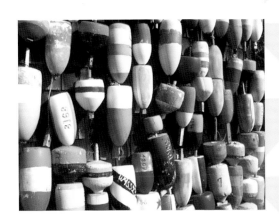

RED/BLUE 3D

As you can see, this optical adventure is nearly over. For your finale, you're going to visit some out-of-this-world places. In order to get there, however, you'll need one more piece of equipment: a red/blue 3D viewer.

Look around. There's a good chance that you have a pair of these red/blue viewers somewhere in your junk pile. Perhaps you bought them with a 3D comic or found them at a museum store? But suppose you don't own a pair? Don't worry, they are easy to build. Here's how.

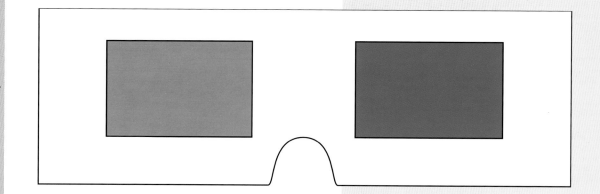

MATERIALS

Heavy-stock paper
Tape
Pair of scissors
Red and blue transparent report covers

TO DO

1. Use a pair of scissors to carefully cut out the viewer frame from a sheet of heavy-stock paper. Make sure that you cut away the two center "windows."

2. Cut out a rectangle of both red and blue plastic. The rectangles should be slightly larger than the frame windows.

3. Use tape to secure the plastic lenses to the frame.

4. Look through these lenses to decode the anaglyphs on the next page.

HINT

If you know someone who works in a theater, ask for two small pieces of blue and red lighting gels.

The Science

The double-printed red/blue (or in some cases red/green) illusions are called anaglyphs (pronounced AH-nah-gliffs). Each image contains a right eye and left eye view. One view is printed in red, the other view in blue. The two views are sandwiched atop each other. The red/blue glasses decode the jumble by sending only one image to each eye. Your brain does the rest.

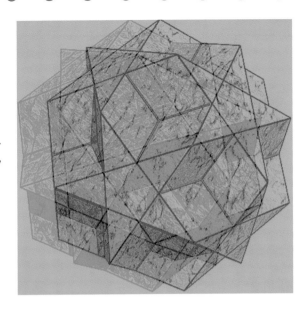

Out of This World Illusions

For our final effect, may we present out-of-this-world images! These anaglyphs were made from stereoimages captured by the Pathfinder spacecraft and beamed back from the surface of Mars!

The anaglyphs presented on these pages are a basic sandwich of a right and left view image.

79

About the Author

Michael Anthony DiSpezio is a renaissance educator who teaches, writes, and conducts teacher workshops throughout the world. He is the author of *Critical Thinking Puzzles, Great Critical Thinking Puzzles, Challenging Critical Thinking Puzzles, Visual Thinking Puzzles, Awesome Experiments in Electricity and Magnetism, Awesome Experiments in Force and Motion,* and *Awesome Experiments in Light and Sound* (all from Sterling). He is also the co-author of over two dozen elementary, middle, and high school science textbooks and has been a "hired creative-gun" for clients including The Weather Channel and Children's Television Workshop. He also develops activities for the classroom guides to *Discover* magazine and *Scientific American Frontiers.*

Michael was a contributor to the National Science Teachers Association's Pathways to Science Standards. This document set offers guidelines for moving the national science standards from vision to practice. Michael's work with the NSTA has also included authoring the critically acclaimed NSTA curriculum, *The Science of HIV.*

Index